Sign Language

KAREN PRICE HOSSELL

Heinemann Library
Chicago, Illinois

© 2003 Heinemann Library
a division of Reed Elsevier Inc.
Chicago, Illinois

Customer Service 888-454-2279

Visit our website at www.heinemannlibrary.com

Page layout by Vicki Fischman
Photo research by Amor Montes De Oca
Printed and bound in the United States by Lake Book
Manufacturing, Inc.

07 06 05 04 03
10 9 8 7 6 5 4 3 2 1

Library of Congress Cataloging-in-Publication Data
Price Hossell, Karen, 1957-
  Sign language / Karen Price Hossell.
    p. cm. -- (Communicating)
Summary: Presents an overview of the history, development,
and functions of sign language, as well as some of the
different kinds of signs that are used.
Includes bibliographical references and index.
  ISBN 1-58810-487-7 (HC), 1-58810-943-7 (Pbk.)
  1. Sign language--History--Juvenile literature. [1. Sign
language--History.] I. Title. II. Series.
  HV2476 .P75 2002
  419--dc21

                    2002001684

Acknowledgments
The author and publishers are grateful to the following for
permission to reproduce copyright material:
Cover photograph by Brian Warling/Heinemann Library
Title page, credits page, pp. 4, 5, 14, 15, 16, 17, 18, 19, 20,
21, 22, 23, 24, 25, 27, 28, 29, 30, 31, 32, 33, 34B, 35, 36,
37, 44, 45 Brian Warling/Heinemann Library; Illustrations
pp. TL all , BR, 12, 13, 26, 29, 31, 47 Micka Klauck; p. 6
Sandro Vannini/Corbis; p. 7 The Granger Collection; p. 8T
Corbis; p. 8B H. Emanuel; pp. 9, 40 Bettmann/Corbis; p.
10T SW Productions/Getty Images; p. 10B S. Grant/TRIP;
p. 11L David Madison; p. 11TR EyeWire Collection/Getty
Images; p. 11BR The Image Bank/Getty Images; p. 34T
Heinemann Library; p. 38 The Kansas State Historical
Society; Illustration p. 39 Carla Kiwior/Wilkinson Studios;
p. 41 Charles E. Rotkin/Corbis; p. 42 Bob Daemmrich/Stock
Boston Inc./PictureQuest; p. 43 Insight Visuals
Communications.

Special thanks to Arika Okrent for her help in the
preparation of this book.

About the consultant
Arika Okrent received an M.A. in linguistics from Gallaudet
University in Washington, D.C. She is currently a Ph.D.
candidate in linguistics and psychology at the University
of Chicago.

Some words are shown in bold,
like this. You can find out what they
mean by looking in the glossary.

Contents

A Silent World 4

The History of Sign Language .6

Signs in America 8

Everyday Gestures 10

The American Manual Alphabet 12

American Sign Language 14

Don't Just Use Your Hands! 16

Features of American Sign Language 18

Special Signs 20

Feelings and Colors 22

People Signs 24

Numbers and Days of the Week 26

Work and Play 28

Clothing Signs 30

Food Signs 32

Animal Signs 34

Putting It All Together 36

Native American Sign Language 38

Everyone Spoke Sign Language Here 40

Careers in Sign Language 42

Signing in Other Countries 44

Glossary 46

More Books to Read 47

Index 48

A Silent World

Imagine a world of silence. You cannot hear your friends say your name. You cannot hear thunder rolling in the sky. You cannot hear music, rain, or laughter.

Deaf people live in this silent world. There are about two million deaf in the United States today. Their lives are much like those of hearing people. Deaf people watch television, go to plays and operas, drive cars, and use computers. They go to school, play sports, and laugh with friends. They get married, have children, and go to work.

The deaf have found a way to communicate. You may have seen them moving their hands and fingers back and forth as they communicate.

Deaf

To make the sign for "deaf," use your index finger to touch your right ear first. Then touch the right corner of your mouth.

Their language may seem mysterious, but it isn't. It is as easy to learn as Spanish, German, or any other foreign language.

The language of the deaf community is called **sign language**. The **hand shapes** they make are called **signs**. Almost anyone can make the signs used in sign language. It takes a lot of practice to learn the signs well enough to talk with a deaf person. But people who know sign language open themselves up to a new way of communicating— one that they can use anytime, anywhere.

Who Uses Sign Language?

There are many kinds of deaf people who use sign language. Some can hear a little, and some cannot hear at all. Some people were born deaf, and some lost their hearing when they were older.

Some people who cannot hear do not know any sign language, but most deaf people do know sign language. They are proud of their language and use it to tell jokes and stories, to tease each other, to argue, and to share secrets. Some deaf people are famous in the deaf community for the beautiful poetry they perform in sign language.

There are also many hearing people who know sign language. Some of them have deaf family members or friends. Some of them have to communicate with deaf people in their jobs. Some of them are just interested in learning a new language and making friends with deaf people!

Speak

With your right hand in the "4" hand shape, touch your index finger to your chin. Move your hand away from your face in a repeated motion.

The History of Sign Language

In ancient times, people who were born **deaf** were treated badly. They did not go to school because people thought they could not learn. In ancient Greece, children who could not hear were sometimes even left outside to die. In ancient Rome, deaf people were not allowed to become Roman citizens. This kind of thinking went on for a long time.

Even while the deaf were being treated this way, **sign language** was being used. Historians have discovered that sign language has been around for many centuries. Deaf people made up **signs** so they could communicate with one another and with hearing people. People in **monasteries** also used sign language. A monastery is a building where **monks** live. Monks are religious men who devote their lives to their religion. Some groups of monks believed that they could concentrate on their religion better if they were quiet. So they almost never spoke. Instead, they developed sign language and used it to communicate.

In the 1500s a wealthy man in Spain asked the head of a local monastery to take in his two deaf sons and try to teach them. A priest at the monastery, Pedro Ponce de León, began to teach the boys using sign language. Many people were surprised when the boys soon learned to read and speak. The priest began to teach more deaf pupils. However, he did not write down how he taught his students. No one is exactly sure how he did it.

For centuries, monks have lived together in monasteries like this one in Cluny, France.

Then another Spanish priest named Juan Pablo Bonet started teaching deaf students using sign language. He wrote about how he taught his students, and this helped others who wanted to teach the deaf. People began to realize that the old ideas about deaf people were false, and that the deaf could learn as well as anyone.

Another priest named Charles Michel, the **abbé** de l'Epée, lived in France during the 1700s. He searched for deaf people so he could learn their signs. He realized that people in the deaf community were already using signs to communicate. He wanted to use the signs to teach French to deaf people. In 1755 he opened a school and used sign language to teach deaf students. Michel also created a dictionary of the signs his students used to communicate. Students learned so much that Michel took them on a tour of the country. People from all over came to see the deaf students read, write, and answer difficult questions about mathematics and history.

Charles Michel's teaching methods became very well known. People from many countries came to France to study how to teach the deaf. Then they went back to their countries and started schools for the deaf.

Charles Michel, who lived from 1712 to 1789, helped develop a way of teaching sign language in France.

Know It

Schools using Charles Michel's methods were started in several countries, including Holland, Poland, Sweden, and Ireland.

Signs in America

A man named Roch-Ambroise Cucurron Sicard taught at the school for the **deaf** that Charles Michel founded in 1755. Sicard was a brilliant teacher and became well known for his work with the deaf.

This is a portrait of Thomas Hopkins Gallaudet, who lived from 1787 to 1851.

Thomas Hopkins Gallaudet, an American, went to hear Sicard speak in London. Gallaudet was traveling around looking for a good way to teach deaf children. His friend's daughter was deaf, and he thought she should have a chance to go to school. Gallaudet liked Sicard's speech and decided to go to Paris to visit Sicard's school. Gallaudet stayed at the French school for two months and then returned to his home in Connecticut. He brought a deaf French teacher with him, Laurent Clerc, because he wanted Clerc to teach **sign language** to deaf people in the United States. Later, Gallaudet married Sophia Fowler, a deaf woman who graduated from his school.

Gallaudet got money from the Connecticut **legislature** to build a school for the deaf. The school,

Today, around 2,000 students attend Gallaudet University in Washington, D.C.

now known as the American School for the Deaf, opened in 1817 in Hartford, Connecticut. Soon schools for the deaf were opening all over the country.

In 1864 Gallaudet's son, Edward Miner Gallaudet, received help from leaders in Congress to open a college for the deaf in Washington, D.C. The school taught using sign language, but in 1868 some of the students were also taught speech and **lipreading.** Now the college is known as Gallaudet University.

When the International Congress on the Education of the Deaf met in 1880, participants decided that deaf children should learn how to talk and lip-read instead of how to use sign language. For about 80 years after that decision, sign language was rarely used to teach the deaf. But in the 1960s, William Stokoe published two books on sign language explaining that it is a true language. Many people started to change the way they thought about sign language. Now it is the most popular kind of **manual communication.**

A Deaf President for Gallaudet

Gallaudet University had always had hearing presidents before 1988. Deaf people were getting advanced education and entering different careers, but they still did not hold many positions of power. When the time came for a new president to be chosen, students felt that a deaf person should hold the highest job at the university.

There were many qualified deaf people for the job, so when the university chose the only hearing candidate to be the next president, students and teachers protested. The protest was a success and a deaf president was selected. I. King Jordan became the first deaf president of the university.

This drawing from the late 1800s shows how sign language was used to teach mathematics at a school for the deaf.

Everyday Gestures

People use their hands to communicate all the time. What do you do when you say good-bye to someone? You wave! In American **culture**, that is the **gesture** for "good-bye."

If you think something is disgusting, you might pretend to stick your finger down your throat. That is a gesture of disgust.

When you stick your thumb up in the air, it means something is good, or that "it's a go." When you point your thumb down, it means that you do not like something, or that something is not going to work.

Placing our hands over our heart and sighing often indicates that we love someone, or that we think a person is pretty or handsome.

When you hold out your hand with your palm facing you and wiggle your fingers back and forth, you usually mean "come here." Sometimes people do that with just their index finger.

Sometimes when we are bored, we make the gesture for yawning, even though we are not really tired.

We use other parts of our bodies to communicate as well. If we raise our eyebrows, for example, we show that we are surprised.

Waving is a gesture that most people use in the United States for either "hello" or "good-bye."

This could mean that something good just happened.

When people shrug their shoulders, they are usually saying "I don't know" or "I don't care." You shake your head back and forth to say "no," and up and down to say "yes."

These movements are a simple kind of **sign language.** But while we use them to show just a few words or ideas, **deaf** people who use sign language put *all* words and ideas into signs.

Sports Signals

If you have ever watched or played sports, you know that referees and umpires use hand signals to guide the game. In football, the referee raises both arms when a player makes a successful touchdown. In baseball, the umpire crosses his arms and moves them back and forth when a player is safe. Below are some sports hand signals and their meanings.

When this signal is made with an umpire's right hand, it means "two strikes."

In football, this signal means a touchdown has just been scored.

When a basketball referee raises their right fist in the air like this, it means there has been a foul.

11

The American Manual Alphabet

The **American Manual Alphabet** has 26 **signs**—one for each letter of the English alphabet. When people sign using the alphabet, they use one sign for each letter to make a word. This is called **finger spelling**.

When people first learn finger spelling, they do it very slowly, and it can take a long time to sign a sentence. But people who have lots of practice at finger spelling do it quickly. They go from one sign to another so fast that some readers may not see all of the signs. But people who are used to finger spelling usually have no problem understanding it. Expert finger spellers use a flowing motion when they sign.

When people finger spell, they hold the first and last signs of a word longer than they do the letters inside the word. That way, the reader knows when one word ends and the next begins.

Your palm should face outward for most letters, and you should try to keep your arm still when you finger spell. Some people hold their right wrist with their left hand to keep it still. If you are left-handed, you can sign with your left hand. You don't have to use your right hand.

The best way to learn to finger spell is to do it in front of a mirror. That way you can see how the signs would look to the person reading them, and you will be able to see if you make a mistake.

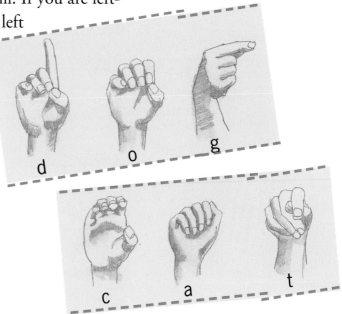

d   o   g

c   a   t

Signs of the American Manual Alphabet

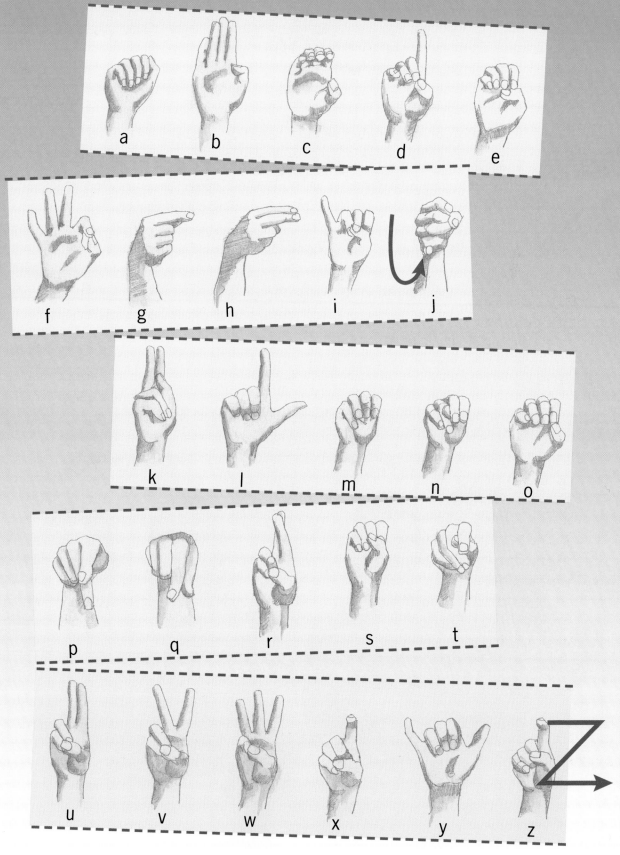

American Sign Language

Probably the most common form of **sign language** used in the United States and Canada is **American Sign Language,** or ASL. The **American Manual Alphabet** is actually part of ASL. This language has its own **grammar** and vocabulary, as well as **dialects** and **slang** expressions. It is called a natural language, which means that the people who use it—members of the **deaf** community—develop it to fit their needs.

American Sign Language became well known after 1964, when a book called the *Dictionary of American Sign Language* was published. Until then, many people thought that sign language was not as good as spoken language. They thought that deaf people should only be taught to speak and read lips. One man who encouraged the use of American Sign Language was William Stokoe, a professor at Gallaudet University

Invite

Thank You

To make the **sign** for "invite," bring your upright, curved palm from the right side of your body down to your waist.

Put the fingertips of your open hand up to your mouth with the palm facing you. Then move your arm down to an angle.

who helped write the dictionary. He showed that signs were not just imitations of actions, but that they were built by putting smaller pieces together—like spoken words are built by putting sounds together.

ASL is not simply signed English words. It is a separate language. In fact, some colleges now include classes in American Sign Language in their foreign language departments.

The Basics

Signs are built out of four smaller parts.

1. **Hand shape:** This is the way you hold your fingers.

2. Location: Every sign must be made in the correct place. Some signs, for example, are made close to the head. Others could be made at the chin, the shoulder, or the chest. In ASL, signs are never made below the waist.

3. Direction: The palm of your hand can face in different directions. It can face away from or toward the body, or it can face upward or downward from the body.

4. Movement: You must be careful to move your hand properly. You often have to move your hands in a particular way to make a sign.

It takes much longer to **finger spell** "snake" than to make the sign for it in American Sign Language.

s   n   a   k   e

Don't Just Use Your Hands!

When you write, you show that you are asking a question by putting a question mark at the end of a sentence. Or you can show surprise by using an exclamation mark. But **sign language** does not have that kind of **punctuation.** Instead, **signers** use their eyes, eyebrows, shoulders, and other parts of their bodies to show things like surprise and anger. Everyone involved in a sign language discussion should do this. By using their bodies to show emotions, signers add meaning to the message. The people reading sign language can use their bodies to show how well they understand the message and how they feel about it.

Facial expressions are important when **signing** and when reading signs. For example, if you smile when you sign something, the person reading your signs will know that you are kidding or happy, or that you think the message is funny.

This is the sign for "think." The facial expression tells you that it means "thinking hard," or "concentrating."

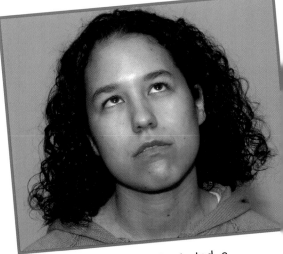

If you are bored or frustrated, a facial expression like this, along with a **hand shape,** will communicate the idea well.

The direction you are looking can give information. A glance at the thing you are talking about can tell the other person what the topic is.

The position of your body can be important. When you ask a question, lean slightly toward the person you are talking to.

Facial Expressions in Sign Language

- If you raise your eyebrows, you show that you are surprised.

- If you squint your eyes, it means that you are thinking about something or that you are puzzled.

- Eye movements are important when signing. If you look over to an object in another area while you are signing, you signal that you are talking about that object.

- You should always keep your eyes on the person who is signing. It is considered rude to look away because it interrupts the signer.

- **Posture** is also important. When you lean forward as you sign, you show the reader that you are asking a question. When you lean away, you show that you do not like what the signer is telling you about.

Features of American Sign Language

Signers use the space around them when they sign. Think of the space in front of you as your signing space.

Pronouns are words such as "he," "she," "it," "we," and "you." When signers talk about someone who is not there, they set up a place in front of them to stand for that person. Then they point to that place to say "he" or "she." When signers point at the person they are talking to, they are indicating the pronoun "you."

Some signs use the space around a signer to stand for something else. For example, with the signs for "past," "present," and "future," the space around the signer stands for different times. The past is behind the signer, the present is where the signer is standing, and the future is ahead of the signer. Other signs use this same time line. The signs for "yesterday" and "last year" move backward and the signs for "tomorrow" and "next year" move forward.

Past

To make the sign for "past," wave your hand over your shoulder with your palm facing backward.

A Different Way of Communicating

There are many situations where we can see better than we can hear, and **sign language** can be a big help in these situations. For example, if you are standing too far away from your friends, they cannot hear your voice. But if they can see you, you can sign to them instead. You can even sign with someone underwater!

Some situations are more difficult for sign language. For example, in the dark or on the telephone, signing does not work because you cannot see the other person. Having enough light in the room is very important for **deaf** people. But they can still communicate in the dark by putting their hands on each others' signs to feel them. This is how people who are both deaf and blind communicate. Deaf people use a teletypewriter, or TTY machine, to communicate by telephone. The TTY machine lets the person type a message that shows up on a screen at the other end. Deaf people also use e-mail and instant messaging for long-distance communication.

Present

Future

The sign for "present," or "now," is made close to the body.

The sign for "future" moves forward from the body.

Special Signs

To show a plural—for example, to make "cookie" into "cookies"—you can do two things. First, you can repeat the **sign** in more than one place to show that you are talking about more than one cookie. You can also show a plural by adding the sign for "many" to the sign you want to make plural.

Some signs, such as the one for "birthday," are actually made up of two signs, just like compound words in English. To show a plural for "birthday," you make the sign for "birth" once, then make the sign for "day" twice.

To show that they feel strongly about something, signers use more force

Many   **Cookies**

To sign "many," curl up your fingers with your palms facing up. Open up your fingers and close them again.

"Many cookies" can be signed by repeating the motion of using a cookie cutter.

to make the sign. Signers usually add a **facial expression** to go along with this. To show that you are very bored, you would make the sign for "bored," then add a facial expression such as rolling your eyes to show just how bored you are.

To sign that you are very excited, you could make the sign for "excited" and smile, or even jump up and down. There is another way of showing degrees of something using the same sign. For example, to sign "very small" instead of just "small," signers change the distance between their hands.

To make a sign **negative**—in other words, to say "no paper" instead of "paper"—signers add the sign for "no" or "not" to the sign for "paper." Signers can also shake their heads to signal "no" or "not."

Birth-   day

"Birthday" is two signs put together. First, sign "birth-" by bringing the back of your right hand down into your left palm.

Then sign "day" by putting your right elbow on the top of your left hand. Swing your pointed right index finger down to your left elbow.

Feelings and Colors

Practice making these **signs** in front of a mirror or in front of another person. Remember to use **facial expressions** to show different emotions. It is like when you make your voice go up and down to show how you are feeling when you speak. A happy or excited face is like a happy or excited voice.

Excited

Happy

Laugh

With palms facing inward and middle fingers slightly bent, make circles in the air.

With your palm facing inward, sweep it upward two times.

Using the "L" **hand shape,** point to the corners of your mouth with your index fingers. As you pull your hands out, curl up your index fingers.

Green

To sign "green," make the hand shape for "G." Then twist your hand back and forth with a small motion in front of your shoulder.

Know It

Many of the color signs use the hand shape for the first letter of the English word for that color.

Blue

Red

Using the hand shape for the letter "B," repeatedly twist your wrist so that your palm moves out.

To sign "red," move your right index finger down from your lips two times.

People Signs

These are some **signs** for the special people in your life. People make these signs differently depending on how old they are. The signs for "grandmother," "grandfather," "sister," and "brother" were originally combinations of two separate signs. Older people still sign them that way. The signs have changed over time into one movement. When babies say "Mama" and "Dada," they point to their chin or forehead with the index finger. This is because babies cannot make the full **hand shape** yet.

Mother

Father

Using the hand shape for the number "5," tap your thumb on your chin.

The sign for "father" is similar to the sign for "mother." Tap your thumb on your forehead instead of your chin.

Grandmother

Begin with the sign for "mother." Then move your hand away from your face with a double arc motion.

Grandfather

This sign begins with the sign for "father." Then move your hand away from your face with a double arc motion.

Sister

Make the hand shapes for "A" with your right hand and "L" with your left hand. Put your right thumb on your cheek. As you swing your right hand down to rest on top of your left hand, straighten your right index finger.

Brother

Make an "A" hand shape with your right hand and an "L" with your left hand. Touch your forehead with your right hand. As you swing your right hand down to rest on top of your left hand, straighten your right index finger.

Numbers and Days of the Week

American Sign Language has **signs** for everything, including numbers.

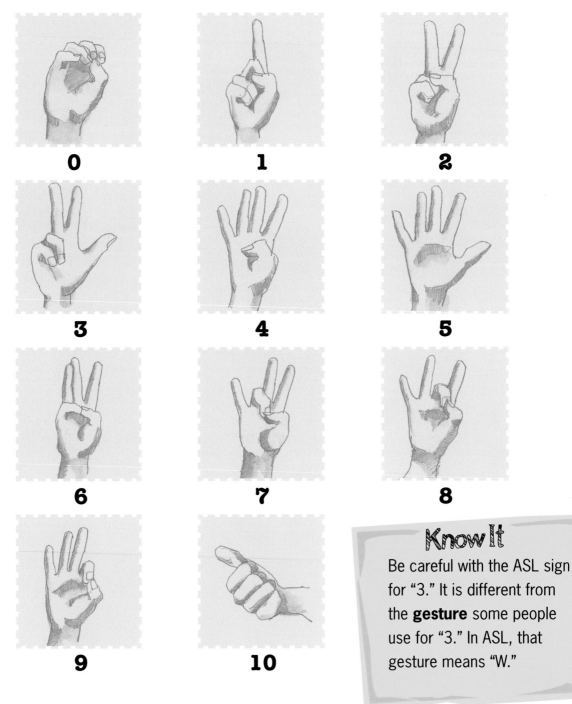

0	1	2
3	4	5
6	7	8
9	10	

Know It

Be careful with the ASL sign for "3." It is different from the **gesture** some people use for "3." In ASL, that gesture means "W."

Days of the Week

As you can see, all of the signs for the days of the week, except "Sunday", are made by signing the first letter of the day in a small circle. "Thursday" is made with the sign for "H" so it does not get confused with "Tuesday."

Sunday

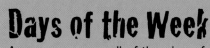

Monday

Tuesday

Wednesday

Thursday

Friday

Saturday

Work and Play

Talking about the things you do during the day is a good way to practice a new language. If there are activities you want to talk about, but you do not know the **signs**, you can look them up in an **American Sign Language** dictionary.

Desk

Tap the top of your right forearm twice with the bottom of your left forearm.

Study

Write

Make the "5" **hand shape** with your right hand. Wiggle your fingers as they point toward your left palm.

Act like you are writing with an imaginary pen on your left palm. Move the "pen" from the heel of the left palm out to the fingertips.

p a r t y

Bicycle

To sign "bicycle," rotate your fists like the pedals of a bicycle.

Game

Swim

Put both hands in the "10" hand shape with the knuckles facing together. Tap your knuckles twice.

Beginning with both palms facing down in front of your chest, move your hands apart as if you were swimming.

Clothing Signs

You may have noticed that sometimes **signs** look like the things they mean. This is true for some of the signs for clothing. For example, the sign for "dress" looks like the shape of a dress on the body. Even though some signs look like what they mean, you still have to learn how to make them. There are many different ways to make a **gesture** that looks like something, but there is only one way to make the correct sign. You could make a gesture for "dress" by waving your hand around like the movement of a skirt, but it would not be the correct sign for "dress."

Begin by making the "P" **hand shape** with both hands. Start at the hips and move your hands up to your waist twice.

Pants

Shoes

To sign "shoes," make the "S" hand shape with both hands and tap them together.

However, there are many signs that do not look at all like the thing they mean. For example, the sign for "shoes" is not made near the feet because that is not a possible location for a sign. The sign for "shoes" is not made by pointing at your shoes, either. You have to make the "S" hand shape with both hands and tap them together. This is very different from what you may have thought!

Dress

Put both of your hands in the "5" position. Bring them up to each side of the top of your chest. Then brush your thumbs down along your body and outward.

Food Signs

You are not supposed to speak with your mouth full. Food gets in the way and makes it hard to understand what you are saying. It is okay to **sign** with your mouth full, though! You can chew with your mouth while you talk with your hands. However, there are situations that make it hard to sign, like when you have your hands full. If you have your hands full, you can still sign with just your fingers, or with one hand. But it is much harder to understand. It is a lot like speaking with your mouth full!

Put the fingers of your right hand together. Then bring your fingertips to your lips.

Eat

Apple

Ice Cream

Make the "X" **hand shape** with your right hand and touch the knuckle to your cheek. Twist your wrist downward twice.

To make the sign for "ice cream," move the thumb side of your fist downward twice, like you are licking an ice cream cone.

Make a "C" hand shape. Start with your fingertips at your chest and move your hand downward.

Hungry

Baby Talk

Some hearing babies have been taught how to use **sign language.** Since they have not yet learned how to speak, their parents teach them a few simple **signs.** These babies can use the signs to communicate with their parents. The babies use sign language to tell their parents that they are hungry, or that they are hot or cold, or that they need medicine. Some of these signing babies are only ten months old!

Soda

Pizza

Make a "Z" in the air with your hand in the "P" hand shape.

Make a fist with your left hand. Put your right middle finger into the fist. Then take your finger out and slap your left hand with your open right hand.

Animal Signs

Here are some fun **signs** for animals. Not only can you sign about animals, but you can also sign *to* animals. If you can train a pet to respond to your voice, you can train them to respond to a sign. For example, a dog can learn to sit or stay when you say "sit" or "stay." But a dog can also learn to sit or stay when you make the sign for "sit" or "stay."

People use many different gestures to communicate with animals.

Cat

Rabbit

Make the "F" **hand shape** with both hands. Then move your fingertips outward from the corners of your mouth a few times.

Using the "U" hand shape, cross your arms above your wrists. Bend your fingers and straighten them twice.

Horse

Put your hands in the "U" hand shape and raise them up to your ears. Bend your extended fingers twice.

Elephant   ## Cow

Make a "B" hand shape with your right hand and put it on the end of your nose. Move your hand down in a wavy motion.

Using a "Y" hand shape, put your thumbs on both sides of your forehead. Twist your hands forward.

Putting It All Together

American Sign Language does not always put words in the same order that we use in English. To say "Have a great day" in ASL, you would usually leave out the "a." **Signers** often leave out **articles** such as "a," "an," and "the." They also leave out other small words. Instead of saying "Nice to meet you," they often sign just "Nice meet you."

Know It

The signs for **pronouns** such as "I," "you," "he," and "she" are only a little different from one another. These signs depend on where you point your finger.

Subjects

I   You   He or She

Actions

Like   Go   Eat

In English, when we want to put special attention on a word, we say it a little louder than the other words. For example, you would say "I didn't go to the MOVIES. I went to the LIBRARY." In ASL, you put special emphasis on a word by moving it to the front of the sentence. So you would sign "Movies, I didn't go. Library, I went." Also, question words go at the end of the sentence. So for "What is your name?" you would sign "Your name what?" Don't worry too much about putting signs in the correct ASL order, though. Even though it can get complicated, most **deaf** people will understand your signs if you put them in the order you are used to.

Practice
You can combine the signs on these pages to make many different sentences. Find out how many ASL sentences you can make.

Things

Mother   School   Ice Cream

A Question

Your   Name   What

Native American Sign Language

Native Americans who lived on the Great Plains, or the middle part of the present-day United States, used **sign language.** The tribes who used sign language included the Sioux, Cheyenne, Blackfoot, and Kiowa. Each tribe had its own language, so these Native Americans signed when they met someone from another tribe.

Native Americans also used sign language when they were on the warpath and sneaking up on their enemy. They used it when they went hunting, too, so they would not scare away the animals.

The **signs** were made at chest level with both hands. However, Native Americans made many signs with only their right hand.

Know It

Thomas Edison filmed Buffalo Bill, a famous cowboy, and Sioux Chief Iron Tail signing in 1898.

Native Americans also used to communicate with settlers and government representatives. The sign being used here by Three Fingers, the Native American man on the left, refers to war paint.

Plains Signs

These signs are different from ASL signs. They are called Plains signs because they were used by Native Americans who lived in the Great Plains. Compare the sign for "horse" in ASL with the Plains sign.

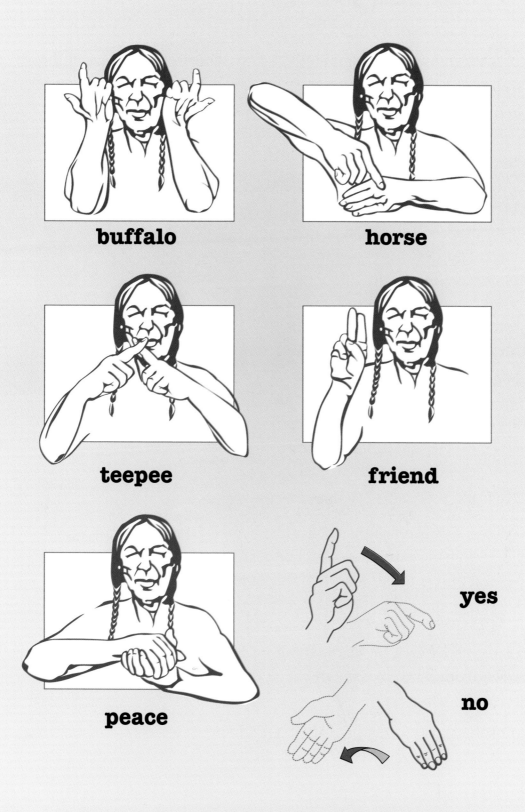

buffalo

horse

teepee

friend

peace

yes

no

Everyone Spoke Sign Language Here

There are some hearing people who know **sign language,** but most hearing people do not. In the 1700s and 1800s there was a place where everyone, both hearing and **deaf,** knew sign language. This place is called Martha's Vineyard, an island off the coast of Massachusetts. There was **hereditary** deafness among the people who lived there. Deafness was passed down through the families, so the amount of deaf people was much higher on the island compared to the rest of the country. In one part of the island, one out of every four people was deaf. This meant that deafness did not seem unusual to anyone. Hearing people learned sign language so that all the people could communicate with each other. Everyone knew the same language.

This 1877 engraving shows a family in Martha's Vineyard. At that time, many residents used sign language.

At that time, deaf people in the rest of the United States could not participate in many parts of society. The hearing society thought that because deaf people could not speak, this meant they were ignorant. Hearing people did not realize that deaf people could speak with their hands. Most deaf people were not allowed to get an education, take part in social activities, or even get married. But on Martha's Vineyard, the deaf ran businesses, participated in government, and had large families.

After the American School for the Deaf opened in Hartford, Connecticut in 1817, almost all of the deaf people from Martha's Vineyard were educated there. They brought their local sign language with them, and it mixed with the French Sign Language being taught at the school. This mixture became the **American Sign Language** of today.

In 1874 President Grant took a vacation in Martha's Vineyard. Before that, the island was unknown to outsiders. But it soon became a popular tourist spot. As the islanders had more and more contact with outsiders, the deaf population started to decrease. Many people moved away to look for better job opportunities, or to marry people from other places. The people who moved to the island did not have hereditary deafness, so fewer deaf children were born on the island. Soon most of the hearing people on the island did not learn sign language any more.

A painter named Thomas Hart Benton spent summers on the island, and in 1926 he made a painting of a deaf couple named George and Sabrina West. They were part of the last generation of deaf islanders. In 1952, the last deaf islander died.

Today Martha's Vineyard continues to be a popular tourist destination.

41

Careers in Sign Language

Sign language can be useful in any career. **Deaf** people interact with people in every profession—including doctors, travel agents, mechanics, salespeople, and many others—to get the things they need.

Sign language can be especially important for teachers, too. Teaching is important for deaf students. Also, people who know sign language work with deaf children and adults in many different places, such as hospitals and museums.

An excellent knowledge of sign language is absolutely necessary to be an **interpreter.** Interpreters act as "go-betweens" for deaf and hearing persons.

Some sign language interpreters are employed by the government. This woman is interpreting at a press conference in Texas.

This teacher is using a game to teach sign language to students.

Interpreters must know a great deal about both sign language and the deaf community. They should know more than one kind of sign language, because not all members of the deaf community use **American Sign Language.**

Interpreting can be hard work. Interpreters have to stand for long periods of time. While they are standing, they hold up their arms to make the **hand shapes** of sign language. And while they are doing that, they must listen closely to the words being spoken so that they interpret everything correctly. It is difficult, but it can also be exciting. Interpreters get to work in all kinds of areas. They interpret meetings, conversations, speeches, and even plays and concerts.

Becoming an Interpreter

People who want to become interpreters should study sign language and use it often. Some colleges and universities offer degrees in sign language interpreting. Professional organizations also offer certifications in the field of sign language interpreting.

Signing in Other Countries

American Sign Language is used in the United States and in English-speaking Canada. But just as there are many spoken languages in the world, there are also many **sign languages.**

International Sign Language is used when people from many countries come together. International Sign Language is used at international events such as the World Games for the **Deaf.** It is called an artificial language, which means that it was created and then taught.

Many countries have their own, different versions of sign language. Some of these versions have common **signs,** while other signs are completely different from those used in other countries. Australian Sign Language, for example, is similar to British Sign Language. But it also has signs that are used in Irish and American sign languages.

Know It

There are many **dialects** in British Sign Language. Someone in Northern Ireland may sign very differently than someone in Scotland.

Travel

Make the **hand shape** for "V" with your palm facing down and curl your fingers a little. Then swing your hand up and forward.

People in Great Britain speak the same language that people do in the United States. But British Sign Language is much different from American Sign Language.

French Sign Language is used by about 100,000 people in France. In 1830 it became the first sign language to be officially recognized as a language. Many sign languages, including American Sign Language, have been influenced by French Sign Language.

Russian Sign Language was first developed in 1806. It also has some similarities to French Sign Language. Russia has had special schools for educating deaf children since 1878.

In Thailand, some of the signs are the same as in American Sign Language. The deaf community in Thailand has several dialects, though, that are very different from one another.

World

Make the "W" hand shape with both hands. Then move both hands forward while making circles in the same direction. Finish the sign with your right little finger on top of your left index finger.

Glossary

abbé French religious leader

American Manual Alphabet signs used in finger spelling; each sign represents a letter or number

American Sign Language language used by many people in the United States and English-speaking Canada

article word like "a," "an," or "the" that is used before a noun

culture beliefs and behaviors of a particular group of people

deaf nonhearing person; often used to refer to all nonhearing people

dialect way of speaking or signing that is particular to a region

facial expression way the face looks when a person feels an emotion

finger spelling communication by signs made with the fingers; each sign stands for a letter or number

gesture movement that expresses an idea or word; this is used by most people and is not considered sign language

grammar system of words within a language that tells how those words should be written and spoken in order to be understood

hand shape movement of the hand to make a sign

hereditary trait or characteristic that passes from parent to child

interpret listen to a person speaking English and convert the message into sign language

legislature group of people with the power to make and change laws

lip-read figure out what someone is saying by watching the movement of their lips and face

manual communication using the hands to communicate

monastery home for people who have taken a religious vow

monk person who has taken a religious vow

negative in language, a statement that includes "not," "no," "none," or "any"

posture way someone holds their body when sitting or standing

pronoun word that substitutes for a noun, such as "he," "she," "it," "you," "we," and "they"

punctuation marks used in writing to make its meaning more clear; punctuation marks include periods, commas, question marks, and exclamation marks

sign hand shape that stands for a letter, word, or idea; also, to use sign language to communicate. A signer is someone who is using sign language.

sign language language that uses the hands to communicate

slang informal word or expression

More Books to Read

Basinger, Carol. *Everything You Need to Know about Deafness.* New York: Rosen Publishing Group, 2000.

Kramer, Jackie and Tali Ovadia. *You Can Learn Sign Language!* Mahwah, N.J.: Troll Communications, 2000.

Olsen, Madeline. *Native American Sign Language.* Mahwah, N.J.: Troll Communications, 1998.

Robson, Pam. *Body Language.* Danbury, Conn.: Scholastic Library Publishing, 1998.

Index

American Manual Alphabet 12–13, 14
American School for the Deaf 41
American Sign Language (ASL) 14–15, 26, 36, 37, 39, 41, 43, 44, 45
ancient Greece 6
ancient Rome 6
animal signs 34–35
Australia 44

babies 24, 33
Benton, Thomas Hart 41
Bonet, Juan Pablo 7
Buffalo Bill 38

Canada 14, 44
careers 9, 42–43
Chief Iron Tail 38
Clerc, Laurent 8
clothing signs 30–31
color signs 23
Connecticut 8, 9, 41

days of the week 27
deaf people 4–5, 6, 7, 8, 9, 11, 14, 19, 37, 40, 41, 42
dialects 14, 44, 45
dictionaries 7, 14, 15, 28
Dictionary of American Sign Language 14, 15

Edison, Thomas 38
email 19

facial expressions 16–17, 21, 22
feelings 16–17, 20, 22
food 32–33
Fowler, Sophia 8
France 6, 7, 8, 45

Gallaudet University 9, 11, 14
Gallaudet, Edward Miner 9
Gallaudet, Thomas Hopkins 8
gestures 10–11, 26, 30, 34
Great Britain 44, 45

history 6–7
Holland 7

Indonesia 41
instant messaging 19
International Sign Language 44
interpreters 42, 43
Ireland 7

King Jordan, I. 9

Martha's Vineyard 40–41
Massachusetts 40
Michel, Charles 7, 8
monasteries 6

Native American sign language 38–39
Northern Ireland 44
number signs 26

people 24–25
play signs 29
plurals 20
Poland 7
Ponce de León, Pedro 6
pronouns 18

Russia 45

schools for the deaf 7, 8, 9, 41, 45
Scotland 44
Sicard, Roch-Ambroise Cucurron 8
slang 14
Spain 6
sports signals 11
Stokoe, William 9, 14
Sweden 7

teletypewriter (TTY) 19
Thailand 45

West, George and Sabrina 41
word order 37
work signs 28
World Games for the Deaf 44